The Inexperienced Midwife

Miceál Kea

ARLEN HOUSE

The Inexperienced Midwife

is published in 2016 by
ARLEN HOUSE
42 Grange Abbey Road
Baldoyle
Dublin 13
Ireland
Phone/Fax: 353 86 8207617
Email: arlenhouse@gmail.com

Distributed internationally by
SYRACUSE UNIVERSITY PRESS
621 Skytop Road, Suite 110
Syracuse, NY 13244–5290
Phone: 315–443–5534/Fax: 315–443–5545
Email: supress@syr.edu

ISBN 978–1–85132–132–2, paperback

Typesetting ¦ Arlen House

The Inexperienced Midwife

Dedicated to
Dennis O'Driscoll
Donal O'Siadhach
Barney McKenna

Contents

Composed

Billions of years before the evolution debate,
skeletal fragments, calcium and other ingredients
came together in a corner of the Calves' Field.

In 2008 in the same corner, I park myself
on their unseen efforts – under the oak
we made into a tree-house –
attempting 'The Dawn Chorus' in G,
during that gorgeous interval
between day and night.

From the top of my hair
to the tips of my toes I know
I'll never play the banjo
like Angelina does.

In truth, I came here to worry.
I think I'm broke. Spent. Dry.
Flittered away all the magic
securing my inheritance.
Freaking out, blood pressure
pent up, requesting freedom.

I am a haemophiliac
fretting in the scale of futile,
like the ground under me
far too stony to notice …

Stealing Kisses

Reality breaks beneath
the drawn purple drapes.
Day creeps along the carpet.
Cruel light divides us equally.
Vampires – the night is ours.

We still have time …
it's not yet now.

Tell Me Your Dreams

It's half past eight, cars are stirring going to work.
I sent you a text at five past one.
Wish I could have whispered it into your ear.
I knew it would be hours before you wake.
A little present. Waiting.

When the gods decide, allow me
to stay over; even then
you're nine foot away, alone in another room.
May as well be a mile past the edge of the universe.
You really need to come out.

Succession

I

On this farm lie the remains of an older farm
and homestead, on what's officially rough grazing.
For greenhorns – that's where more rocks
than grass grow,
where we out-winter just-weaned calves,
which has me here now
with a bale of black-wrapped stew.

Parts of this corpse are more living
than others. Her house still intact,
bar the roof, of course.
Amazingly-crafted dry walls,
no draft even today.
The rest, reminders –
a decomposing photograph.

Mud sticks. So do names,
when asked who lived there?
Nancy – I'm, probably, positive
Dad made that up.
But every place is called something
even if it's just the meadow on the right.

II

A skeleton of a road travels through
these five acres of limestone and few
hardy blades, then corners right
down to the village.
In the other direction it can be traced
through four fields; where in the corner
of the furthest field over
another neighbour lies in state.

Was this road a compulsory purchase perhaps?
An upgrade to deal with the increased
heavy goods asses? Clogging. Disputed.

Did Nancy protest? Maybe
with battle looming,
promised by the feudal chief,
returning warriors? Extraneous,
and set the table for round-bale feeders.

III

Land doesn't die, it just changes hands.
In February I planted cabbages
under a tunnel in her house.
Didn't take much to water
– one can from the neighbouring turlough.
By the time I'm squishing caterpillars,
carrots, spuds and onions will have, hopefully,
moved in. I'll be drawing barrels then.

May not be much now
but every chop starts life as semen.
This is the second time I've tried this,
to grow from ruins. And all I've learnt since
wouldn't be half a sentence in a college textbook
– a lot of it's luck,
and potter home in my chariot
a king.

Neé Linnane

I

Gran

Never burnt her bra.
Always had the kettle boiled
and the sweets well hidden.

She loved her High Nelly
would cycle down to Sweeney's in Mulroog
or Lane's of Toureen for tea and talk.

Now she time-travels, chases shadows,
meandering trails carved over mountains
generations deep.

II

Grandmother Clock

Originally from Carron, County Clare,
then hung on the wall at Aunt May's in Pollock,
went to Toureen and finally in Creglucas
was placed on the wall – just
as the leaves began to fall.

The year our constitution was born
she was nineteen years ticking.
Six more years of flawless timekeeping
my father arrives into this world.
Sixty-four years later I turn twenty seven.

In her 89th year at 5.21 am
gathered around her hospice cell
choking on our anger, smoking cigarettes,
trying to beat her to it. Back home
in the hallway the clock stops dead.

III

The Removal

Mick, Matty, Jimmy and Frank stand –
the four moons of this dead Sun.
The two remaining daughters
burka-black on comfortless chairs.

Alzheimers may have relieved her of many things.
But Micheal McTigue stealing her banbh.
That, she refused. Even after
the lid is screwed on.

* The ace of hearts in the card game 25 is called the Banbh (Bonham).

Israel and Palestine are now Friends on Facebook

You like this

Sitting behind yere walls. Comfortable.
Trolling. Expert. Posting stones.
Let them fall, please. It breaks
our windows, lets in the rain.
We board them up, we are blind.

And wet.
Oh brothers of stars; soil and flesh
that buries and loves –
it's not fair, children growing up
knowing only funerals.

Yere: Abbas and Netanyahu.

Midwifery

She looks at me
licking her cold heap of nothing.
Lengths of rain come down
on grass and concrete –
it does not discriminate.

Standing there I think that's cruel.
We have hands to hold,
cradle into the tit.
What good are four legs
when your child is dying in front of ewe.

ARRANGEMENTS

1

We arrive on the scene.
Single white car; crumpled.
Tears of glass for two broken bodies,
the jaws of life cannot fix.
Rain falls on orange flashing.

2

Our bedroom door lies open.
In the kitchen, the wedding present radio
regurgitates – impending economic doom;
some *Big Brother* nobody is pregnant;
a car crash; the continuing threat
posed by Iran …

3

The red rocking horse
bought for her fourth birthday.
The sole survivor.

Trad Session, O'Connor's

I am the only carnivore
among tenth-level vegans.
They start *Tripping up the Stairs*
as I tumble down the stairs.

I ravage my steak
as everyone else
picks up *The Blackthorn Stick*
and twirls it about effortlessly
as I exsanguinate myself in C natural.

Walking on Water

Out across the turlough, hack and sledge
fishing – small buckets filling big barrels.
Thirteen days the water pump has been on strike.
Thankfully, Minus 13 is extremely bipolar …

A living ecstasy of concrete soil and glass.
Each blade, branch and rock
erotically clad in white balaclavas.
I know it's them. I can see their eyes.

VILENICA CAVE: CLOSING CEREMONY

Vilenica Festival, Slovenia

We gather – like the leaves will soon –
schizophrenics from all over the world.
Clouds crack'd: a shimmering spectacle.
Day and night chase each other about.
Captivating in leaps and bounds, we interpret
and rotate. Celestial bodies, casting shadows
on individual leaves of surrounding saplings.

The dancers disappear.
A hand reappears, beckons
us down
          to
             the
                 depths
                           we
               descend
        the
steps.
Where we find the two lovers dancing,
this time, with the sun and the moon
and music soliloquys around them.
Fixated as the stalactites, I stop.

This is where they used to come to read,
when verbs were illegal and metaphors
a death sentence. The cold would mute
to communists' ears. I am uncomfortable,
the wren.

DR ZOONOTIC

Zoonotic, a disease of the animal transferrable to man

I know that ewe has maggots
and I can cure until the next time.
My eyes have radar. I can see them.
The little blithers wriggling, nibbling.
Eating her alive. She has the look:
head-heavy. Stretched low and long;
hoping they'll fall out her mouth.
She has no hands to squish them,
pick them off. She can't speak to the flies,
ask them not to laid their eggs
in her incubator wool.

ACORNS

for Jennifer

In my weaker moments I pity them; then I remind myself they're here to teach – Bart Simpson

I

This one's for you, Miss Kealy.

But did you actually expect us to learn anything,
double English first thing every Monday morning?
Even more poignant: you died before
I could share my *Inheritance* with you.

Miss Sweeney waltzed into class one day
with a tape of Beethoven and Mozart
and their Magic Flute.
Laughing out our arses,
Murphy swore blind he had one.
By the end of the class I begged her
to borrow the tape.

The things we did to the student teachers –
reducing one to tears.
God how we laughed at that,
sneaking a quick fag in the jacks,
hoping Stan wouldn't come in
with his notebook and pen.

We had other teachers
who taught *yer father*
and who knew well where the line was
straight across the side of your head.
Then there was those bi-polar ones –
horrible forty-minute periods

when we quickly learnt what
we could get away with.

Those types of lessons aren't taught.

II

Some weekend a memory ago
a gang of us decided to camp
at the back of the school.
We weren't even drunk,
but it seemed like a good idea, at the time.

Vodka, Bulmers and Miller.
Drink Aware – ha.
What the fuck did we care,
we were teenagers and it was 1997.

We lit a fire. Scared
and it burnt the world around us.
But had it all planned. Exactly.

We pulled a placard of Bertie
off a telegraph pole,
took turns pissing on his Haughey-esque grin.
Prophetic, if he only knew
in less than ten years
two of us would be married
and one of us dead.

III

The day we were let out of the pen,
that day we got our results.
Those all important
pieces of toilet paper.
We went to Kinvara to celebrate.
Yes, I said Kinvara.
We pushed the boat out.
Bought champagne; £30 –
the euro isn't that old.

But neither were you.

The Adventures of Nigel Kingdom

I

Sitting on a beach
disintegrating with worry
wondering why I'm wet.

In my pocket, a rubric cube of maggots
small enough to fit into a box of cigarettes.
I only pretend to smoke so no one will see it.
Twisting, pock-marking my skin,
letting me know it's still there.
If I could scream, I think
leaves would shatter.

Concrete ships anchor to my feet,
tide tickling my lungs.

II

I normally take the ferry to prison.

My attempt to prove God's existence
didn't sit too well with our blasphemy laws.
Chain-ganged with other sinners
I pretend to dress as a wolf,
paranoid about sheep, breaking rocks.
It's always fifty eight degrees, even in the rain.
Boss never sweats.
Behind his cinematic shades
my duty and dreams fight.
Paroled home at weekends, a recovering alcoholic
on a daytrip to the brewery. Temporary
I tell myself, the elephants in every room.
Scenes unfold in cute surround sound.

But not today, I can't. I have to do this
or I'll go mad, dying.
My heart will always be green. And hers.
International is local: somewhere else.

III

Not quite Neil Armstrong –
but the plank is on the way,
followed by tourists.
Not me. *One way* –
I tell your one behind the glass,
pointing to the destination I can't pronounce.

Rattling over sleepers; a passenger sneezes.
Outside a bird startled to fright
rises up, wingspan making midday midnight,
lifts the train clear, wriggling in its talons.
I should've fastened my seatbelt.
Through sky like a stone,

the air, slippery.
Couldn't grab hold of the clouds.
Ground approaching, not making way
and that was the last train, ever.
Deliberately chosen
so I couldn't return.

HOME FROM REHAB

Not even Sam's shadow
follows her in.
The place all to herself.
The phone rings.

She lights another cigarette.

Sam will answer it
if they call back.
Something
to look forward too.

DEPRESSING COMPANY

When my skin itches, normal time speeds up.
I'm unaffected, plod along as normal.
There's no music when this happens.
Just an itch. I'll never be able to scratch
this living, wriggling black
maggot under folds of skin.

Weighing an imperial ton.
I want it gone. X-rays and MRI's
show the doctors nothing –
shadows disappear in the light.
So what drug can they dispense?

They're times I operate on myself,
desperate to relive. Pull it out.
Never on the face are exits cut –
people would see. Then ask.
Between your toes, your armpits.
Best places are well hidden under clothes.

All post-op results reveal
it's resident in my marrow
and no amount of chemo will kill
this part of my shadow, lurking
just out of sight.

The Gardai have the power to take you into custody,
if they believe you have a mental disorder –
and they did.
ECT will help you get better.
Most patients recover from a mental disorder
within the first few weeks; some take longer.

We'd be playing fun when the knocks
or telephone calls came.
Always at night. We looked forward to them.
Holidays.
Not that we didn't care.
We were never told anything, ever.

Sundays were quiet, long car journeys
in itchy mass clothes to state-of-the-art
Victorian buildings, bull bar windows
and retina scanner doors.
You may want to leave, you can discuss this
with a member of your care team.

Sitting strange in smoke-flavoured big rooms,
out-of-date crosswords and padded pens,
tablets and lies falling out your ears.
I'll be back soon – here?
ECT will help you get better.

We were never told anything, ever.
Any wonder the apple grew on the breast?

THE NIGHT'S EVENTS

In a creepy cold attic
laughing and joking with Santa
lies the Red King.
Time is there too
and we play with the Moon
on creaky old floorboards –
the Tooth Fairy, the Easter Bunny,
even the monster-under-the-bed comes out.

Sharing the night,
a support group for the bereaved.
When alarm clocks below
wake the world they vanish,
leaving time. Taking a shard
from the window pain
bleeds out into day.

The Three Stooges

Fishing trips in Connemara,
all night PlayStation sessions,
skulling pints in Jordan's.

When we drank all our money,
hitched to the ATM in Kilcolgan
– there are still charges pending.

Musical instruments
which could not hold a tune,
though we knew how to play
each other.

Late one September evening
Kieran and myself were informed
we were to be uncles. That night
Larry, Curly and Moe
drank the last of the summer wine.

APRÈS DINNER

Gran's grey watering can,
my nephew Jamie uses it
to store the frogs he collects.
Sure we did the same: the amount
that got stuck in the spout, died
and had to be poked out with a stick.

She bought it from a tinker
decades before Dad was born.
Officially worthless. I use it this evening
to water the cabbages,
down upon the caterpillars, squatting,
followed by my thumb.
The dog runs about mad as I walk
back and forth, filling from the blue barrels.

I have one more job that I can do
practising a few reels.
My fingers do not need my eyes
so I make myself a voyeur.
In the woods, where they cannot see me –
watchin' who's bullin' – the snakes among the cows.

Years and years of the same tractor traversing
the same tracks have left undulating cleats,
slithering towards the three gates below in the field
where I soon plan to introduce a fourth.
I'm afraid the snakes will bite me
if I do it wrong.

Thus Taught Teagasc

I

C.I.A.
(Certificate in Agriculture)

Franciscan Brothers Agricultural College,
Mountbellew – the latest crop of post-emergence
Tadagh's.

Green-Cert's follow me.
We cautiously creep
along unfamiliar hallways.
Photographs of past classes hang,
people I don't know, including
these fifty five weanlings.

Roll call, *anseo.*
The principal wears his matching smile
with his welcoming tie. Teachers take turns
like the leader-follower system
we'll later learn. Modules the buzz word.
115 credits, the magic number.

II

THUS TAUGHT TEAGASC

And we underline passages from our textbooks –
wasting the ink in our highlighters …

Food Conversation Efficiency;
Economic Breeding Index;
1st Service Interval;
Land Parcel Ratios
and % D.M.D.

Now, that's all good and well
and quite the mouthful – calculators
don't get TB.

III

THE 2009 NATIONAL PLOUGHING CHAMPIONSHIP

A zoo of intersecting metal grids,
ex-ministers and fortune tellers.
Tents of cattle that Tick All The Write Boxes.

Machinery being molested
like a dog at Crufts.
I feel sorry for the Brazilian model
standing front of house. Poor girl,
she'd be more comfortable at a cocaine party,
not shivering size zero in a field in Kildare
smiling out leaflets for a hay-turner
worth a hundred-and-forty-nine grand.
How much for a hayfork
and a few good neighbours?

I see giddy calves following kids,
chasing lambs – priceless –
and finish off my burger.
In the next quill an old man shears
without a machine. Fully dressed,
no marks, no cuts. No sweat.
His eyes sown deep in furrows,
just like Dad.

I wait with the ache
of never-going-to-be-read booklets of bullshit.
School kids light fireworks and cigarettes.
I was here before; Offaly, Transition Year.
Funny, the parts of you, you lose.
Find, destroy. Exchange. Today
I have 47 credits.

IV

INTEREST

I'm currently learning about soil
form Vinny Flynn. It's interesting
how modern technology can help:
composition, structure, reference charts, apps.

The type you have determines
what you can do best – ha.
Ya hear that Heaney, ya hack,
yourself and that other stony auld sod.

My studies to date with Rita Hughes
in cash accounts – the particulars
of labour costs and believe me,
the irony is banked.

CROSS
College Days

Minusing what I owe
from what I need, equals
net. Of course, full of holes.
Other necessary smoke-ables –
lol ... paid for by the State.

Jim the roommate burnt his sausages
the other day, blacker
than the starving black babies
Gran would point to on the Trocaire box
to get me to eat the burnt bits I didn't like.

How do you burn sausages?
Or for that matter, any food
to the point it becomes inedible?
We're both from farming stock
– *ya wouldn't give that to the dog.*
And he didn't. Binned.

It's not long before he's thirsty
and flies out the door, Amen.
Then I open the fridge
beneath the sink.

Same Sex

It's something truly fantastic,
secretly held love –
pure heroin in virgin veins.

We came out
in McDonagh's fish and chips shop.
Held hands above the table

and lips. Some diners didn't care.
Others said *Uh* … and finished off
their haggis.

The Rock

What draws me up today? Sheep!
Counting them – easier to find a ghost
among the oceans of gorgeous limestone,
islands of ash and evergreen, holly and hazel.
Nettles and ferns higher than yourself.
The original décor, before the rib was taken out.

32.46 hectares – Google Earth told me that.
Every autumn we'd ramble up the Rock,
empty yellow manure bags under our arms,
to the slit with every hazelnut in sight.
Never once a thought for the squirrels.

No more than the lambs and calves,
we were weaned too.
The bags were discarded like droppings
between the cracks. Waiting.
Decomposing into paint.

I lived up there for a while.
Collected stones, stockpiling
dung and bones, creating
my own fields first until I realised
I needed real ones. Where
I found a lead balloon

harpooned by the Hawthorns.
I followed its tail – tangled, strangled,
twirling through spongy deep moss.
The wind is without bias
towards sheds
and kites.

The Pursuit of Happiness

If I can see her, can she see me?
The way I do, the moon incarnate.
God I want to tell her. My tongue
ready, set in concrete.
But my arms aren't.

The letters come like the rain,
the distance that separates us.
Experiences, adventures, desires
shared on A4. Dull are my days
when the dog doesn't bark – postman's here.

Our love map birthed on Libra's scales.

Would you like to meet?
I wait and wonder nervously,
how you'll have your hair.
A few months later
after the news *Crimewatch* recalls
my last known movements.

AMEN

Extreme deliveries deprive oxygen,
but hallowed be the Red Lamp
placing the lamb on my lap.
He's slow at first, but soon finds second gear
and discovers he's the throttle to back it up.
Eyes loud. Tiny tongue sucks,
pucks the tit right off the bottle.
I've seen this before, despite
all his attempts the jelly in his legs
will never set. It's a hard journey to make,
into the shed – to get the sledge.

Pay and File

The fatter the leg
the more cumbersome the waltz
around the shed, dizzy
trying to out-step the other.
I work up a sweat handing sheep to Seán.
Dad packs away their coats.
Shepherds and hawthorns grow one way,
crook'd.

Shearing starts, obviously, with talk
until the first click of the cord
setting blades a-munching.
The first nude looks tiny, interfered with almost –
quickly swallowed up by the rest of the clouds.

Betwixt clicks and oil spurts
they talk about places that, Jesus,
even Google couldn't find. Refer to men
from out back that way –
Sure wasn't he always like that.
Chuckle, chuckle, chuckle …

Then mention methods and practices
that Teagasc trendsetters suited behind desks
couldn't even spell, let alone fathom.
I need thirteen more credits to complete
my Advanced Certificate in Agriculture.
Chuckle, chuckle, chuckle …

LARRY AND BARRY

A Galway and Suffock ram
employed on our farm
to fuck.

When the midwife is due
Larry and Barry are left to themselves
and two in to Alpha doesn't go.

Over the years I witnessed
every business blow,
reduced blood
from torrent to trickle.

When Larry developed meningitis
he was taken into care,
Barry had a look
that struck me dumb.

I will never be able to tell Barry
I was there
when life left his body.

A mountain crumbling into nothing.

A Better Understanding

I

Pealing out of the day's stale skin.
Paper-thin disguises
suspended on hangers.
Tickets into other worlds.
Who am I now –

naked before the mirror
bleeding on floorboards kissing
in tongue and groove.
My curtains are polka dot blue.
A chameleon. I am changed.

I wonder how many people
stop for the wind.

II

Slamming tonight in Limerick, the All Ireland.
The White House the closest I'll ever get.
Though I could be related,
my name is Kearney. Irregardless,
the wheel of night advances.
It is October brilliant bright
and the moon is giddy, runs on before me
as I tear through the fields
*ar mó tairbh bán** with my offering
of yet-to-be-realised words.
My communion
for wounded tongues.

* The White Bull of Connacht

III

The juxtaposition of metaphors
and why it's not really about the curtains,
even though it is, doesn't translate too well
when you're speaking French
to someone from Mars.
Tell that to the aunts, whose tongues
would sharpen scythes. Let's see
how they like being transvestites.

There's times I like to laugh –
Leaving Cert's worrying whether or not
I'm … going to come up. Have to explain
the use of my modifiers
and 'were the curtains really blue?'

Ha. I am Muslim –
no more than the sausages
I've never not eaten.

Thorns

Close my eyes, a surprise
you say you have,
and stand there grinning
like the ass you are – an application form
for the Rose of Tralee. No less.

My precious, you may be the boss
of those animals out in the fields
but we know exactly who has the final say.
Don't we?

I will gladly cook your dinner,
in her kitchen under her eye and tongue.
Thank you for the thought and effort
but I will not win
until she is dead.

Stag Night

It began with a bang,
the taking of a life.
Collecting the body, the car
would alert to our crime.

Gran fell back the land once,
sat in and wheeled home.
They don't make wheelbarrows
like that anymore.

Next time, we'll use a rifle,
shotguns are messy.
Chewing on pellets
ruins the venison.

Tea Time

It takes four hours to cut, bale and wrap
the three meadows.
The first headland wouldn't be cut
in that length. I'd go back with tea
and paper sandwiches. A dessert
being in their shade.

I never did grow enough
to wield the scythe.
Lucky. I was told. Horsepower
lessened men. And horse.
But there was time for tea.
There's always time for tea.

To celebrate the saving
there'd be a gathering.
Frank Joe would produce his fiddle,
the women dance. It was magic
and rich. The closest to expressing our feelings
and us kids allowed to stay up.

It's one man doing all the work today.
One man called John Deere
who has no time for tea.

SUBURBIA

Does the sower/sow by night/
or the ploughman in darkness plough?
– William Blake

On this night
black as innocence lost,
buses, taxis, airplanes
plough with broken furrows
the fields of Castleknock, Dublin 15
where after the wind from a bottomless bag
disperses the tears
of every parent shed
to fall on disturbed tarmac.

Before the rays of the sun
make pale the moon
and extinguish street light,
with junkie's needle
and rotting reed, blot
in moon black blood
this balcony where I make myself scarecrow
keeping a watchful eye
for all the children taken.

The Department of Suicide Prevention

After Dave Lordan
For Brian

You woke early, I'd say,
rope ready, it's what I would have done
so not to disturb anyone
then slipped into something more comfortable

naked as the snowdrops.

THANKS FACEBOOK

Rape crisis director Rachel,
I've put seven clients your way. Eight soon.
Laura posted new photos.
A barbie in the back garden.

She's apt with the lens,
makes my job a piece of cake
and I like
each deliciously-detailed slice.

Low back wall, trees either side.
Bushes galore. Perfect. And the cherry,
no searchlight above the patio door.
The small things mean so much to me.

After I'm done with her, Rachel,
I'll devote and volunteer all I can,
to get my timing and the layout.
It'll make a fantastic headline.

Long Distance

Until you are in my arms, for real
we make do with Nokia
delivering letters, tiny
envelopes of flutters.
And capital Xs.

From our window made of stars
we chat, exchange emoticons
our hands desire to touch,
connect, minus the URL.

But thanks Mark
for bringing the moon
that little bit closer.

Mark Zuckerberg, Facebook

GMT
1:40 in the afternoon,
in my kitchen making tea,
Galway Bay FM playing Joe Walsh
Life's been good to me –
'I have a Maserati, it does 185
I lost my licence …'

We interrupt with news just in:
Benazir Bhutto is dead.
More on this story in our next news bulletin.

Stir in the final half spoon of sugar.
Dunk a custard cream. Silly cow.
That was never going to work.

'… I lost my licence
now I don't drive'.

Hidden Hearing

Anyone sitting here?

Five minutes ago
we were thrusting in the toilets.

Our clothes take the stance
of opposing forces. Your alibi.
Tongues become texts.
I always have credit when in character.
Every get-away-able touch of flesh
a trillion-volt surge of lust.
We go to mass
just to shake hands.

Our eyes transfixed,
the place could be burning down
and all the love letters won't change the fact
that I cannot read and you cannot write.

Ah grief, my old friend –
I love drowning in your company.
After a decade, I'm still
diving in, to sink in concrete shoes.
Momentary. Fleeting, nice
like masturbating to an ex.

What the virgins and policy makers
will never understand, the money spent –
small things. Harmless, delicious, little shiny things.
Supporting. Fuelling.
You never hear about that, your honour.

But gravity is crueller,
levels drop, evaporate to nothing.
The immigration of ecstasy,
naked and dripping dry.
Grieving.

Mileage

Early in the am,
my insignificant blue car
exits off this roundabout
onto a stretch of road
that council workers made
with picks and shovels. They toiled,
dug, leveled, tarmac-ed and painted,
readied this road for such a purpose
and I don't know what their grievance is
but they take umbrage at my presence tonight.
Lined either side, poised like lampposts –
lingering ephemerals with shovels,
picks and sledges, just waiting
for me to pass
in my blue convertible.

I'll never regret walking this road
with flowers for you.

The Clough Road

Led little feet to school.
Anonymous cars would stop, offer lifts.
Abduction … we learnt that in class
along with subtraction.

Buail Liom, Bóg Liom agus
an bhfuil chead agam?
The draughty auld play shelter,
the smooth chalk trees,
learning tables with Mr Mahon
I got many a clip in the ear.
I stole Emmett Divilly's second Capri Sun
every day for over a year,
watching the F.B.D Milk Rás
and trying not to laugh as we sang out of tune
in Ballinderreen National School.

There's very few fields now
not growing tarmac
with lego-brick walls.
Aurinia saxatilis hanging baskets.
A blight.

The night we waked Gran
in Jordan's pink pub
I didn't know her well enough to stay
so walked the road home. One mile
to my bedroom door.

Legacy

She stands up and stabs me
in the eye with the cut of her figure.
I follow her out for a smoke.
Back between noisy bottles and empty glasses
she casually informs me
what she did as a teenager
in front of the mirror.

We laugh, she complains of the weather
then asks, *would you like me to come with you home.*
She adds with a wink, *pun intended.*

Yes, oh God, yes.

With the passing of a moon
arrives an envelope, with a stick.
Positive –

Thanks for the passport,
Mr Poet Man.

WORSHIP

We stood. In the wind.
Hushed. Two trees. Planted
in different ages.

About the Author

Miceál Kearney, 36. Living and working on the family farm in the West of Ireland. Started writing in 2001. Published and performed his poems all over Ireland; America, the UK, Europe and broadcast on radio in Australia. His debut collection was *Inheritance* (Doire Press, 2008). *The Inexperienced Midwife* is his second collection – a journey from A to B via the other 25 letters. He has also published short stories and writes plays; two of which *Never Ending Wild Stories* and *Incestors* have been staged with a third, *Make Me,* due next year. He has been known to play the banjo and is notorious for arguing with vegans on Facebook about the colour blue.

Acknowledgements

The author wishes to thank the editors of the following journals where these poems appeared, often in earlier versions:
'Stealing Kisses', 'Tell Me Your Dreams' and 'The Pursuit of Happiness' in *Envoi;* 'Israel and Palestine are now Friends on Facebook' and 'Pay and File' in *The Blue Max Review;* 'Gross' and 'Stag Night' in Revival; 'Thorns', 'Three Stooges' and 'Suburbia' in *Orbis;* 'Vilenica Cave', 'Tea Time' and 'All the King's Men' in *Crannóg;* 'Larry and Barry' in *Cyphers;* 'The Night's Events' in *The Poetry Bus Magazine;* 'Amen' in *Live Encounters;* 'Arrangements' and 'Midwifery' in *Episteme.*

The poem 'Same Sex' is used in an augmented reality poetry tour of Galway city.

Special thanks to Alan Hayes for his tireless work. And to Sarah Clancy, Kate O'Shea, Mary Mullen, Jan Fortune and Brendan Murphy and all the others who helped create this. To Gene and Margo Barry and the Blackwater International Poetry Festival for all their support. My family and friends. And a big thanks to the slurry; may not be nice but it does make the grass grow.